THE RUINS OF TIME

The Ruins of Time

Antiquarian and Archaeological Poems

Edited by
ANTHONY THWAITE

ELAND • LONDON

This arrangement, preface and postscript © Anthony Thwaite

ISBN 0 907871 98 4

First published in October 2006 by Eland Publishing Ltd,
61 Exmouth Market, London EC1R 4QL

Pages designed and typeset by Antony Gray
Cover Image: Portico of the Great Temple at Baalbec
by David Roberts © Walker Art Gallery, Liverpool
Cover designed by Katy Kedward
Printed and bound in Spain by GraphyCems, Navarra

Contents

PREFACE   9
The Ruin   10
EDMUND SPENSER   12
The Ruines of Time   12
SIR THOMAS BROWNE   14
JAMES CAWTHORN   15
WILLIAM COWPER   17
The Progress of Error   18
PERCY BYSSHE SHELLEY   19
Ozymandias   19
JOHN KEATS   20
Ode on a Grecian Urn   20
WILLIAM WORDSWORTH   23
from *Guilt and Sorrow*   23
Roman Antiquities   24
ARTHUR HUGH CLOUGH   25
from *Amours de Voyages*   25
THOMAS HARDY   26
In the Old Theatre, Fiesole   27
A. E. HOUSMAN   28
On Wenlock Edge   29
JOHN MEADE FALKNER   30
Selibra Cineris Coacta Cani   30
EDWARD THOMAS   34
Swedes   34
Digging   35

RUDYARD KIPLING 36

The Roman Centurion's Song 36

The Land 38

W. H. AUDEN 41

Roman Wall Blues 41

PHILIP LARKIN 42

An Arundel Tomb 42

SEAMUS HEANEY 43

Punishment 44

TED HUGHES 45

Thistles 46

GEOFFREY HILL 47

Merlin 47

Mercian Hymns: I 47

STUART PIGGOTT 49

Ballade to a Prehistorian 50

Congress of Archaeological Societies 51

AGATHA CHRISTIE 52

FLEUR ADCOCK 53

Proposal For a Survey 53

U. A. FANTHORPE 56

Unfinished Chronicle 56

PETER DIDSBURY 59

Words at Wharram Percy 59

ANTHONY THWAITE 61

Monologue in the Valley of the Kings 61

The Return 63

Archaeology 67

Sigma 69

POSTSCRIPT 71

INDEX OF FIRST LINES 75

INDEX OF POEM TITLES 77

ACKNOWLEDGEMENTS 78

Preface

An archaeological dig and writing a poem have a lot in common. Both are searches for meaning, sifting through material that isn't always certain and stable, apt to disintegrate. 'Archaeology – a career in ruins': I first saw this jest on a poster in the office of an archaeological unit. But there is a more romantic view of the minutiae of the past, of the indestructible fragments. As Proust wrote in the early twentieth century:

> Archaeologists and archivists are now showing us . . . that nothing is ever forgotten or destroyed, that the meanest circumstances of our lives, the details most remote from us, have carved themselves into the huge catacombs of the past where humankind records its life-story, hour by hour . . . Whether near or far, in our recent past or back in prehistory, there is not a single detail, not a single circumstance, however futile or fragile it may appear, that has perished.

This anthology is an attempt to bring together a range of responses to the past in verse, from the solemn and sententious sense of fallen glories evoked by Edmund Spenser in the sixteenth century to the more cynical judgement of Fleur Adcock in the present day. 'Sermons in stones' alternate with evocations of particular places, objects, remains. The distant past is brought to life in the brilliant mimicry of Kipling or Auden, or brooded on elegiacally by Housman or Larkin. These poems are full of secrets, lessons, warnings. Egypt, Greece, Rome, from prehistory to the medieval – all are here, commemorated in words that are meant to last.

ANTHONY THWAITE

The Ruin

Laments for the lost past, elegies which follow the theme of *sic transit gloria mundi*, are commonplace. The Anglo-Saxon poet who composed *The Ruin*, which gazes in wonder at the remains of Roman Bath, was part of an old tradition.

> Splendid this rampart is, though fate destroyed it,
> The city buildings fell apart, the works
> Of giants crumble. Tumbled are the towers,
> Ruined the roofs, and broken the barred gate,
> Frost in the plaster, all the ceilings gape,
> Torn and collapsed and eaten up by age.
> And grit holds in its grip, the hard embrace
> Of earth, the dead departed master-builders,
> Until a hundred generations now
> Of people have passed by. Often this wall
> Stained red and grey with lichen has stood by
> Surviving storms while kingdoms rose and fell.
> And now the high curved wall itself has fallen . . .
> Resolute masons, skilled in rounded building
> Wondrously linked the framework with iron bonds.
> The public halls were bright, with lofty gables,
> Bath-houses many; great the cheerful noise
> And many mead-halls filled with human pleasures,
> Till mighty fate brought change upon it all.
> Slaughter was widespread, pestilence was rife,
> And death took all those valiant men away.
> The martial halls became deserted places,
> The city crumbled, its repairers fell,
> Its armies to the earth. And so these halls
> Are empty, and this red curved roof now sheds
> Its tiles, decay has brought it to the ground,

Smashed it to piles of rubble, where long since
A host of heroes, glorious, gold-adorned,
Gleaming in splendour, proud and flushed with wine,
Shone in their armour, gazed on gems and treasure,
On silver, riches, wealth and jewellery,
On this bright city with its wide domains.
Stone buildings stood, and the hot stream cast forth
Wide sprays of water, which a wall enclosed
In its bright compass, where convenient
Stood hot baths ready for them at the centre.
Hot streams poured forth over the clear grey stone,
To the round pool and down into the baths . . .

Anonymous

In the early modern period, Edmund Spenser's lament for Verulamium (now St Albans), first published in 1591 as part of *The Ruines of Time*, is typical.

Here are five stanzas:

FROM

The Ruines of Time

It chauncéd me oneday beside the shore
Of siluer streaming *Thamesis* to bee,
Nigh where the goodly *Verlame* stood of yore,
Of which there now remaines no memorie,
Nor anie little moniment to see,
By which the trauailer, that fares that way,
This once was she, may warnéd be to say.

I was that Citie, which the garland wore
Of *Britaines* pride, deliuered vnto me
By *Romane* Victors, which it wonne of yore;
Though nought at all but ruines now I bee,
And lye in mine own ashes, as ye see:
Verlame I was; but what bootes it that I was
Sith now I am but weedes and wastfull gras?

O vaine worlds glorie, and vnstedfast state
Of all that liues, on face of sinfull earth,
Which from their first vntill their vtmost date
Tast no one hower of happiness or merth,
But like as at the ingate of their berth,
They crying creep out of their mothers woomb,
So wailing backe go to their wofull toomb.

To tell the beawtie of my buildings fayre,
Adornd with purest golde, and precious stone;
To tell my riches, and endowments rare
That by my foes are now all spent and gone:
To tell my forces matchable to none,
Were but lost labour, that few would beleeue,
And with rehearsing would me more agreeue.

High towers, faire temples, goodly theaters,
Strong walls, rich porches, princelie pallaces,
Large streetes, braue houses, sacred sepulchers,
Sure gates, sweete gardens, stately galleries,
Wrought with faire pillours, and fine imageries,
All those (O pitie) now are turnd to dust,
And ouergrowen with blacke obliuions rust.

But antiquarianism perhaps began in Britain round about the middle of the following century. Sir Thomas Browne, the Norwich physician who wrote *Urne Burial*, was a pioneer in this. His *Concerning Some Urnes found in Brampton-Field in Norfolk, anno: 1667*, published in 1683, has been called 'possibly the first excavation report'. In *Urne Burial* his prose is close to poetry:

> Unto these of our Urnes none here can pretend relation, and can only behold the Reliques of these persons, who in their life giving the laws unto their predecessors, after long obscurity, now lye at their mercies. But remembering the early civility they brought upon these Countreys, and forgetting long-passed mischiefs, we mercifully preserve their bones and pisse not upon their ashes.

The Society of Antiquaries of London at one time in the eighteenth century used to meet at the Mitre Tavern in Fleet Street; and there is an interminable set of verses called *Tom's Tale: Understanding with Virtue*, composed by James Cawthorn (1719–1761), about a meeting at which one of the company ('A dean who understood / All that had passed before the Flood') produces 'a dirty copper coin', which is passed from hand to hand. The first antiquary pronounces it to be Roman, with 'that fine domestic scene / When the first Brutus nobly gave / His freedom to the worthy slave'. The next scorns this, and says:

> this little piece
> Is certainly a child of Greece:
> Th' Aerugo has a tinge of blue
> Exactly of the Attic hue . . .
> My eye can trace, divinely true,
> In this dark curve a little Mu:
> And here, you see, there seems to lie
> The ruins of a Doric Xi . . .

But then 'Swinton, full of fire, / Asserted that it came from Tyre . . . a true Phoenician'.

> The next, a critic, grave and big,
> Hid in a most enormous wig . . .
> Wondered that men of such discerning
> In all the abstruser parts of learning,
> Could err, through want of wit or grace,
> So strangely in so plain a case:
> 'It came', says he, 'or I'll be whipt,
> 'From Memphis in the Lower Egypt . . .

'Sir, I'm as sure as if my eye
Had seen the artist cut the die,
That these two curves which wave and float thus,
Are but the tendrils of the Lotus,
Which, as Herodotus has said,
Th' Egyptians always eat for bread.'

And so on – a sort of laborious satire on typology and its errors.

James Cawthorn

By the late eighteenth century, the literary attitude to antiquari-
anism, or 'a taste for the Antique', seems to have hardened. This is
the time of the Grand Tour, when young men of means would travel
round Europe during what we would now call their 'gap year'.
Here is a passage from William Cowper's *The Progress of Error*:

FROM

The Progress of Error

From school to Cam or Isis, and thence home;
And thence with all convenient speed to Rome,
With reverend tutor clad in habit lay,
To tease for cash and quarrel with all day;
With memorandum-book for every town,
And every post, and where the chaise broke down;
His stock, a few French phrases got by heart,
With much to learn, but nothing to impart
The youth, obedient to his sire's commands,
Sets off a wanderer into foreign lands.
Surprised at all they meet, the gosling pair
With awkward gait, stretched neck, and silly stare,
Discover huge cathedrals built with stone,
And steeples towering high, much like our own;
But show peculiar light by many a grin
At popish practices observed within.
　　Ere long some bowing, smirking, smart Abbé
Remarks two loiterers that have lost their way;
And always being primed with *politesse*
For men or their appearance and address,
With much compassion undertakes the task
To tell them more than they have wit to ask;
Points to inscriptions wheresoe'er they tread,

Such as, when legible, were never read,
But being cankered now and half worn out,
Craze antiquarian brains with endless doubt;
Some headless hero, or some Caesar shows –
Defective only in his Roman nose;
Exhibits elevations, drawings, plans,
Models of Herculanean pots and pans;
And sells them medals, which, if neither rare
Nor ancient, will be so, preserved with care.
    Strange the recital! from whatever cause
His great improvement and new light he draws,
The squire, once bashful, is shamefaced no more,
But teems with powers he never felt before:
Whether increased momentum, and the force,
With which from clime to clime he sped his course
(As axles sometimes kindle as they go),
Chafed him, and brought dull nature to a glow;
Or whether clearer skies and softer air,
That made Italian flowers so sweet and fair,
Freshening his lazy spirits as he ran;
Unfolded genially and spread the man;
Returning he proclaims by many a grace,
By shrugs and strange contortions of his face,
How much a dunce that has been sent to roam
Excels a dunce that has been kept at home.

Dismissive though that is, there was at the same time, or almost
the same time, a sensibility that – for quite other ends – looked
towards the distant past for lessons, and took them seriously.

That well-known student dissident, Percy Bysshe Shelley, though he was a considerable traveller, never actually travelled to Egypt; but something he read, in the work of a Greek historian of the Roman period, Diodorus Siculus, helped to give him the *donnée* for his sonnet *Ozymandias* – a poem which manages equally to be antiquarian and political:

Ozymandias

I met a traveller from an antique land
Who said: 'Two vast and trunkless legs of stone
Stand in the desert. Near them, on the sand,
Half sunk, a shattered visage lies, whose frown,
And wrinkled lip, and sneer of cold command,
Tell that its sculptor well those passions read
Which yet survive, stamped on these lifeless things,
The hand that mocked them and the heart that fed.
And on the pedestal these words appear:
"My name is Ozymandias, king of kings:
Look on my works, ye Mighty, and despair!"
Nothing beside remains. Round the decay
Of that colossal wreck, boundless and bare
The lone and level sands stretch far away.'

What Shelley *had* seen, before he wrote that poem, was the recently unveiled effigy of Ramses II in the British Museum in 1818. And here I have to say that for many years I've been bothered by that famous poem by Keats, *Ode on a Grecian Urn*. The poem was written in May 1819. But – what *is* this object? And *where* is it? It's known that Keats made a drawing of the outline of the so-called 'Sosibios' vase (which was then in the Musée Napoleon in Paris), probably from an engraving Keats saw in Henry Moses's *A Collection of Antique Vases, Altars, Paterae . . . etc* (1814). But the closely-described pot itself . . . ? No one seems to know what or where it is.

One supposition which seems to be widespread is that this is a cinerary urn, an urn for ashes. But there's not a single clue in the Keats poem that this is so, and one knows in all kinds of other (typological, historical) ways it can't be so; but I've heard and read several famous literary scholars and commentators on Keats asseverate that this object is a cinerary urn. For me, that's not only wrong, it has nothing to do with the point of the poem – however one might choose to paraphrase that.

Ode on a Grecian Urn

Thou still unravish'd bride of quietness,
    Thou foster-child of Silence and slow Time,
Sylvan historian, who canst thus express
    A flowery tale more sweetly than our rhyme:
What leaf-fringed legend haunts about thy shape
    Of deities or mortals, or of both,
        In Tempe or the dales of Arcady?
What men or gods are these? What maidens loth?

What mad pursuit? What struggle to escape?
    What pipes and timbrels? What wild ecstasy?

Heard melodies are sweet, but those unheard
    Are sweeter; therefore, ye soft pipes, play on;
Not to the sensual ear, but, more endear'd,
    Pipe to the spirit ditties of no tone:
Fair youth, beneath the trees, thou canst not leave
    Thy song, nor ever can those trees be bare;
        Bold Lover, never, never canst thou kiss,
Though winning near the goal – yet, do not grieve;
        She cannot fade, though thou hast not thy bliss,
    For ever wilt thou love, and she be fair!

Ah, happy, happy boughs! that cannot shed
    Your leaves, nor ever bid the Spring adieu;
And, happy melodist, unwearièd,
    For ever piping songs for ever new;
More happy love! more happy, happy love!
    For ever warm and still to be enjoy'd,
        For ever panting, and for ever young;
All breathing human passion far above,
    That leaves a heart high-sorrowful and cloy'd,
        A burning forehead, and a parching tongue.

Who are these coming to the sacrifice?
    To what green altar, O mysterious priest,
Lead'st thou that heifer lowing at the skies,
    And all her silken flanks with garlands drest?
What little town by river or sea-shore
    Or mountain-built with peaceful citadel,
        Is emptied of its folk, this pious morn?

And, little town, thy streets for evermore
    Will silent be; and not a soul, to tell
        Why thou art desolate, can e'er return.

O Attic shape! fair attitude! with brede
    Of marble men and maidens overwrought,
With forest branches and the trodden weed;
    Thou, silent form! dost tease us out of thought
As doth eternity: Cold Pastoral!
    When old age shall this generation waste,
        Thou shalt remain, in midst of other woe
Than ours, a friend to man, to whom thou say'st,
    'Beauty is truth, truth beauty, – that is all
        Ye know on earth, and all ye need to know.'

Wordsworth couldn't really be said to be a poet devoted to antiquities or the remote past; but in his *Guilt and Sorrow; or Incidents upon Salisbury Plain* he prefaced the poem with an 'Advertisement' which drew attention to the circumstances in which it was written, in 1793–94:

> The monuments and traces of antiquity, scattered in abundance over that region, led me unavoidably to compare what we know or guess of those remote times with certain aspects of modern society, and with calamities, principally those consequent upon war, to which, more than other classes of men, the poor are subject . . .

This is stanza XIV of the poem's seventy-odd stanzas:

> Pile of Stone-henge! so proud to hint yet keep
> Thy secrets, though that lov'st to stand and hear
> The Plain resounding to the whirlwind's sweep,
> Inmate of lonesome Nature's endless year;
> Even if thou saw'st the giant wicker rear
> For sacrifice its throngs of living men,
> Before thy face did ever wretch appear,
> Who in his heart had groaned with deadlier pain
> Than he who, tempest-driven, thy shelter now would gain.

Much later, in the early 1830s, Wordsworth wrote a sequence of poems, many of them sonnets, called *Yarrow Revisited, and Other Poems*, which includes several concerned with the antiquities of the Lake District:

Roman Antiquities

(*From the Roman Station at Old Penrith*)

Now profitless the relics that we cull
Troubling the last holds of ambitious Rome,
Unless they chasten fancies that presume
Too high, or idle agitations lull!
Of the world's flatteries if the brain be full,
To have no seat for thought were better doom,
Like this old helmet, or the eyeless skull
Of him who gloried in its nodding plume.
Heaven out of view, our wishes what are they?
Our fond regrets tenacious in their grasp?
The Sage's theory? the Poet's lay? –
Mere Fibulae without a robe to clasp;
Obsolete lamps, whose light no time recalls;
Urns without ashes, tearless lacrymals!

In his verse novel *Amours de Voyages,* written in the late 1840s, Arthur Hugh Clough created a character, Claude, who visits Rome and who finds it disappointing ('Rubbishy seems the word that most exactly would suit it'). In one of his first letters to his friend Eustace, Claude goes on:

> Rome disappoints me still; but I shrink and adapt myself to it.
> Somehow a tyrannous sense of a superincumbent oppression
> Still, wherever I go, accompanies ever, and makes me
> Feel like a tree (shall I say?) buried under a ruin of brick-work.
> Rome, believe me, my friend, is like its own Monte Testaceo,
> Merely a marvellous mass of broken and castaway wine-pots.
> Ye gods! what do I want with this rubbish of ages departed,
> Things that Nature abhors, the experiments that she has
>   failed in?
> What do I find in the Forum? An archway and two
>   or three pillars.
> Well, but St Peter's? Alas, Bernini has filled it with sculpture!
> No one can cavil, I grant, at the size of the great Coliseum.
> Doubtless the notion of the grand and capacious and
>   massive amusement,
> This the old Romans had; but tell me, is this an idea?
> Yet of solidity much, but of splendour little is extant:
> 'Brickwork I found thee, and marble I left thee!' their
>   Emperor vaunted;
> 'Marble I thought thee, and brickwork I found thee!'
>   the Tourist may answer.

The great age of archaeological and antiquarian discovery was of course after Wordsworth, Shelley and Keats – when we get to Petra (that 'rose-red city half as old as time') and to the excavations of Layard at Nineveh, Schliemann at Troy, Sir Arthur Evans at Knossos, Howard Carter and Tutankhamen . . . And this is when we begin to get poems which are, perhaps, archaeological more than antiquarian. Professionalism, of a sort, had arrived. But first Thomas Hardy. Hardy was well aware that he lived on an ancient site. In 1884, he gave an account of *Some Romano-British relics found at Max Gate, Dorchester*: he modestly stated that 'as the subject of archaeology is one to a great extent foreign to my experience, my sole right to speak upon it at all, in the presence of the professed antiquarians around, lies in the fact that I am one of the only two persons who saw most of the remains *in situ*, just as they were laid bare, and before they were lifted up from their rest of, I suppose, fifteen hundred years.' In 1887, on holiday in Italy, he harked back to his Dorchester home, Max Gate (or *Porta Maxima*, as he once put it facetiously to his friend Edmund Gosse). He was several thousand miles from home:

In the Old Theatre, Fiesole

I traced the Circus whose gray stones incline
Where Rome and dim Etruria interjoin,
Till came a child who showed an ancient coin
That bore the image of a Constantine.

She lightly passed; nor did she once opine
How, better than all books, she had raised for me
In swift perspective Europe's history
Through the vast years of Caesar's sceptred line.

For in my distant plot of English loam
'Twas but to delve, and straightway there to find
Coins of like impress. As with one half blind
Whom common simples cure, her act flashed home
In that mute moment to my opened mind
The power, the pride, the reach of perished Rome.

I have to say that I have met both the immediately past tenants
of Max Gate and the present ones; and in answer to my question
about finding Roman coins in the garden or round about, both
families say No, they've never found anything. Perhaps Hardy
had swept up the lot.

As I have suggested, archaeology (not an exact science, but better than what had gone before) began to take over from antiquarianism in the late nineteenth/early twentieth century. And poetry benefited. For one thing, there was Sigmund Freud. Freud wasn't just the pioneer of how to look at and comment on the whole complex business of the human psyche: he was also an almost obsessive and well-informed collector of antiquities, particularly when he moved to Hampstead from Vienna. Freud visited Pompeii in 1902, and already had found that 'archaeology in general provided a useful metaphorical explanation' for what he was doing in the consulting room.

As a much more recent commentator has put it (Jennifer Wallace, in *Digging the Dirt: The Archaeological Imagination*, 2004): ' . . . archaeology itself is often a displacement for other concerns. The act of excavation is centrally bound up with all sorts of cultural anxieties and desires'.

The late nineteenth and earlier twentieth centuries are enormously rich in providing poets of the time with archaeological images and metaphors, and subject-matter in general. Think of A. E. Housman, emotionally stuck in the borders of Shropshire and Worcestershire, brooding over Uricon:

On Wenlock Edge

On Wenlock Edge the wood's in trouble;
    His forest fleece the Wrekin heaves;
The gale, it plies the saplings double,
    And thick on Severn snow the leaves.

'Twould blow like this through holt and hanger
    When Uricon the city stood:
'Tis the old wind in the old anger,
    But then it threshed another wood.

Then, 'twas before my time, the Roman
    At yonder heaving hill would stare:
The blood that warms an English yeoman,
    The thoughts that hurt him, they were there.

There, like the wind through woods in riot,
    Through him the gale of life blew high;
The tree of man was never quiet:
    Then 'twas the Roman, now 'tis I.

The gale, it plies the saplings double,
    It blows so hard, 'twill soon be gone:
To-day the Roman and his trouble
    Are ashes under Uricon.

Much less well known as a poet, though well enough known as
the writer of two novels, *Moonfleet* and *The Lost Stradivarius*,
there's John Meade Falkner, in his Maiden Castle poem –
written in 1885, before Mortimer Wheeler's 1930s excavations.
The title translates as 'reduced to half a pound of white ash':

Selibra Cineris Coacta Cani

He slept beneath his mound of earth
    Alone for eighteen hundred years;
Through centuries of death and birth,
    The counterchange of joy and tears.

They laid him in his lonely bed
    One August night – the sun had set;
They put the pitcher by his head,
    His arrows and his amulet.

Along the short down turf the dew
    Fell heavy, in the vales beneath
The beech-woods loomed in misty blue,
    And on the stream a silvery wreath

Of white night fog hung spiritwise,
    When that strange gathering climbed the down,
Of women with their weeping eyes,
    And bearded warriors weather-brown.

Wild voices rose in mournful choir,
    That echoed on across the sward,
Of children weeping for their sire,
    A people wailing for their lord.

His locks beneath his brazen crest
   The fitful night air moving caught,
And there was buried in his breast
   The Roman pike-head broken short.

And here they made his resting place,
   Beneath the height of harvest moon,
Whence reaching far the eye may trace
   The fosse and rampart of Mai-dún.

They laid the stone across his breast,
   And banked it round with new-cut sods,
That so his spirit might find rest
   From battle with the resting gods.

The moon shone white upon the dead,
   And all the turves with dew were wet;
They put the pitcher by his head,
   His arrows and his amulet.

                *   *   *

The thyme and harebell flowered above,
   The turf grew green above his head;
Nor Roman victor dared to move
   The silence of the resting dead

For eighteen hundred years – and now
   We lie at fall of August eve
And watch below with sweating brow
   These antiquaries toil and heave.

The livelong hours their echoes woke
   The silence of the dreaming day;

With delving spade and pickaxe stroke,
    And mattock cutting through the clay.

The orange haze begins to rise
    That heralds in the harvest moon;
There loom against the southern skies
    The fosse and rampart of Mai-dún.

'Tis time to go, the night is nigh,
    The western light has paler grown;
And as we turn one gives a cry,
    The tool has struck against a stone.

Then spades are busy in the breach,
    The centre of the tumulus;
And eager hands are stretched to reach
    The lid of the sarcophagus.

A moment's space we gaze upon
    The ruins of a Celtic bust,
The white limbs of the skeleton,
    And then they crumble into dust.

Poor chief! and so his frame was spared
    The last indignity of death,
To lie with bones set fair and squared,
    With glass above, and cloth beneath,

In some museum hall, a prize
    Of fallen faiths and people gone,
For rustic loons with open eyes
    To gape and gaze and laugh upon.

*   *   *

John Meade Falkner

I rambled through our new-built hall,
    That magazine of country lore,
From press to press and stall to stall,
    And marked a case beside the door,

All neatly framed and painted brown,
    And over it this legend set:
'Celtic remains from Martinstown,
    Three arrow heads and amulet.'

And there is Edward Thomas, whose poem *Swedes* digs so accurately into the Egyptian excavations of the period, just about the time of the First World War, in which Thomas was killed in 1917 – though, rather as in the case of John Meade Falkner's poem, Thomas's poem precedes the famous discovery of Tutankhamen in 1922:

Swedes

They have taken the gable from the roof of clay
On the long swede pile. They have let in the sun
To the white and gold and purple of curled fronds
Unsunned. It is a sight more tender-gorgeous
At the wood-corner where Winter moans and drips
Than when, in the Valley of the Tombs of Kings,
A boy crawls down into a Pharaoh's tomb
And, first of Christian men, beholds the mummy,
God and monkey, chariot and throne and vase,
Blue pottery, alabaster, and gold.

But dreamless long-dead Amen-hotep lies.
This is a dream of Winter, sweet as Spring.

In another poem, Thomas contemplates the continuity of a simple action. In one of two poems to which he gave the title *Digging*, he finds in a trivial, random act (digging, and finding in the earth two clay tobacco pipes, one of them an abandoned pipe of his own, the other an eighteenth-century pipe) a moment of time which, in an instant, goes back far into the past and reaches forward into the future. He wrote it in 1915, a time when the fields of western Europe were full of trenches dug for war.

Digging

What matter makes my spade for tears or mirth,
Letting down two clay pipes into the earth?
The one I smoked, the other a soldier
Of Blenheim, Ramillies, and Malplaquet
Perhaps. The dead man's immortality
Lies represented lightly with my own,
A yard or two nearer the living air
Than bones of ancients who, amazed to see
Almighty God erect the mastodon,
Once laughed, or wept, in this same light of day.

The levels of this poem are, in a literal sense, the levels of earth which make up the past – and those levels will be added to and will make up the future. In ten lines, Thomas spans remote prehistory (the long-extinct mastodon, seen by our palaeolithic ancestors), the less exotic but still remote past (given precision by the use of those place-names of early eighteenth-century battles), the present moment in which he enacts the title of the poem, *Digging*, and a future into which he too will be stratified as bones, as relics of the past.

Here, perhaps, is the place to bring in Rudyard Kipling. To many of us, now in our sixties and seventies, I suppose Kipling was a sort of tutelary poet of our childhoods and our inclination towards the study of the past. But I have to say, quite honestly, that when I was a boy (and a boy very devoted to the past – to coins, and sherds, and museums, and all the rest of it), I was quite put off by all the Kipling stuff my father thrust in front of me. It has taken a longish time for me to recognise that Kipling was a genius and not an embarrassment. Well, in a way he *is* an embarrassment, but he's a genius as well, particularly where 'relating to the past' is concerned. There are many poems from which to choose, but I have settled first on *The Roman Centurion's Song*:

The Roman Centurion's Song

(Roman Occupation of Britain, AD 300)

Legate, I had the news last night – my cohort ordered home
By ship to Portus Itius and thence by road to Rome.
I've marched the companies aboard, the arms are
                              stowed below:
Now let me take my sword. Command me not to go!

I've served in Britain forty years, from Vectis to the Wall
I have none other home than this, nor any life at all.
Last night I did not understand, but, now the hour
                              draws near
That calls me to my native land, I feel that land is here.

Here where men say my name was made, here where
                              my work was done,

Here where my dearest dead are laid – my wife – my
                              wife and son;
Here where time, custom, grief and toil, age, memory,
                              service, love,
Have rooted me in British soil. Ah, how can I remove?

For me this land, that sea, these airs, those folk and
                              fields suffice.
What purple Southern pomp can match our changeful
                              Northern skies,
Black with December snows unshed or pearled with
                              August haze –
The clanging arch of steel-grey March, or June's long-
                              lighted days?

You'll follow widening Rhodanus till vine and olive lean
Aslant before the sunny breeze that sweeps Nemausus clean
To Arelate's triple gate; but let me linger on,
Here where our stiff-necked British oaks confront Euroclydon!

You'll take the old Aurelian Road through shore-descending
                              pines
Where, blue as any peacock's neck, the Tyrrhene Ocean shines.
You'll go where laurel crowns are won, but – will you e'er forget
The scent of hawthorn in the sun, or bracken in the wet?

Let me work here for Britain's sake – at any task you will –
A marsh to drain, a road to make or native troops to drill.
Some Western camp (I know the Pict) or granite Border keep,
Mid seas of heather derelict, where our old messmates sleep.

Legate, I come to you in tears – My cohort ordered home!
I've served in Britain forty years. What should I do in Rome?

Here is my heart, my soul, my mind – the only life I know.
I cannot leave it all behind. Command me not to go!

Another of Kipling's themes is that of endless recurrence, the way in which the past repeats itself in different ages and through repetition of circumstance. This is what lies behind *The Land*, through the 'thirty generations' of Hobden:

The Land

When Julius Fabricius, Sub-Prefect of the Weald,
In the days of Diocletian owned our Lower River-field,
He called to him Hobdenius – a Briton of the Clay,
Saying: 'What about that River-piece for layin' in to hay?'

And the aged Hobden answered: 'I shall remember as a lad
My father told your father that she wanted dreenin' bad.
An' the more that you neeglect her the less you'll get her clean.
Have it jest *as* you've a mind to, but, if I was you, I'd dreen.'

So they drained it long and crossways in the lavish Roman style –
Still we find among the river-drift their flakes of ancient tile,
And in drouthy middle August, when the bones of meadows show,
We can trace the lines they followed sixteen hundred years ago.

Then Julius Fabricius died as even Prefects do,
And after certain centuries, Imperial Rome died too.
Then did robbers enter Britain from across the Northern main
And our Lower River-field was won by Ogier the Dane.

Well could Ogier work his war-boat – well could Ogier wield
                                                  his brand –
Much he knew of foaming waters – not so much of farming land.

So he called to him a Hobden of the old unaltered blood,
Saying: 'What about that River-piece, she doesn't look no good?'

And that aged Hobden answered: ' 'Tain't for *me* to interfere,
But I've known that bit o'meadow now for five and fifty year.
Have it *jest* as you've a mind to, but I've proved it time on time,
If you want to change her nature you have *got* to give her lime!'

Ogier sent his wains to Lewes, twenty hours' solemn walk,
And drew back great abundance of the cool, grey, healing chalk.
And old Hobden spread it broadcast, never heeding what was in't.
Which is why in cleaning ditches, now and then we find a flint.

Ogier died. His sons grew English – Anglo-Saxon was their name –
Till out of blossomed Normandy another pirate came;
For Duke William conquered England and divided with his men,
And our Lower River-field he gave to William of Warenne.

But the Brook (you know her habit) rose one rainy autumn night
And tore down sodden flitches of the bank to left and right.
So, said William to his Bailiff as they rode their dripping rounds:
'Hob, what about that River-bit – the Brook's got up no bounds?'

And that aged Hobden answered: ' 'Tain't my business to advise,
But ye might ha'known 'twould happen for the way the valley lies.
Where ye can't hold back the water you must try and save the sile.
Hev it jest as you've a *mind* to, but, if I was you, I'd spile!'

They spiled along the water-course with trunks of willowtrees
And planks of elms behind 'em and immortal oaken knees.
And when the spates of Autumn whirl the gravel-beds away
You can see their faithful fragments iron-hard in iron clay.

*   *   *

Georgii Quinti Anno Sexto, I, who own the River-field,
Am fortified with title-deeds, attested, signed and sealed,
Guaranteeing me, my assigns, my executors and heirs
All sorts of powers and profits which – are neither mine nor theirs.

I have rights of chase and warren, as my dignity requires.
I can fish – but Hobden tickles. I can shoot – but Hobden wires.
I repair, but he reopens, certain gaps which, men allege,
Have been used by every Hobden since a Hobden swapped
                                      a hedge.

Shall I dog his morning progress o'er the track-betraying dew?
Demand his dinner-basket into which my pheasant flew?
Confiscate his evening faggot under which the conies ran,
And summons him to judgement? I would sooner summons Pan.

His dead are in the churchyard – thirty generations laid.
Their names were old in history when Domesday Book was made.
And the passion and the piety and prowess of his line
Have seeded, rooted, fruited in some land the Law calls mine.

Not for any beast that burrows, not for any bird that flies,
Would I lose his large sound council, miss his keen amending eyes.
He is bailiff, woodman, wheelwright, field-surveyor, engineer,
And if flagrantly a poacher – 'tain't for me to interfere.

'Hob, what about that River-bit?' I turn to him again,
With Fabricius and Ogier and William of Warenne.
'Hev it jest as you've a mind to, *but*' – and here he takes command.
For whoever pays the taxes old Mus' Hobden owns the land.

Rudyard Kipling

We are now well into the twentieth century, and we reach W. H. Auden. Auden was perhaps first more of a geologist than an archaeologist (it was certainly a boyhood ambition of his to have something serious to do with lead-mines), but, among all his copious and various poems, one of my many favourites is a piece Auden wrote for a commission – a bit of radio poetry, done for a programme in the late 1930s, for D. G. Bridson at the BBC. Auden apparently got much of his inspiration for this programme from reading R. G. Collingwood, whose book *Roman Britain* was first published in 1932. Auden's radio documentary was called *Hadrian's Wall*: it was broadcast in November 1937, with incidental music by Benjamin Britten. From it, this is *Roman Wall Blues*:

Roman Wall Blues

Over the heather the wet wind blows,
I've lice in my tunic and a cold in my nose.

The rain comes pattering out of the sky,
I'm a Wall soldier, I don't know why.

The mist creeps over the hard grey stone,
My girl's in Tungria; I sleep alone.

Aulus goes hanging around her place,
I don't like his manners, I don't like his face.

Piso's a Christian, he worships a fish;
There'd be no kissing if he had his wish.

She gave me a ring but I diced it away;
I want my girl and I want my pay.

When I'm a veteran with only one eye
I shall do nothing but look at the sky.

Philip Larkin, one of whose literary executors I am, isn't much thought of as a person interested in archaeology; but in fact one of his best-known poems is an evocation of a medieval monument which still stands in Chichester Cathedral. Later, Larkin was made aware that he'd got the position of the hands – left and right – muddled up; and, worse, he discovered that the clasped hands weren't medieval at all but a Victorian restoration. Still, it's a great poem, which moves towards a masterpiece of not saying exactly what you want him to say. In another famous poem of his, *Church Going*, Larkin wrote disparagingly of 'some ruin-bibber, randy for antique': I've always ruefully thought I was that very person.

An Arundel Tomb

Side by side, their faces blurred,
The earl and countess lie in stone,
Their proper habits vaguely shown
As jointed armour, stiffened pleat,
And that faint hint of the absurd –
The little dogs under their feet.

Such plainness of the pre-baroque
Hardly involves the eye, until
It meets his left-hand gauntlet, still
Clasped empty in the other; and
One sees, with a sharp tender shock,
His hand withdrawn, holding her hand.

They would not think to lie so long.
Such faithfulness in effigy

Was just a detail friends would see:
A sculptor's sweet commissioned grace
Thrown off in helping to prolong
The Latin names around the base.

They would not guess how early in
Their supine stationary voyage
The air would change to soundless damage,
Turn the old tenantry away;
How soon succeeding eyes begin
To look, not read. Rigidly they

Persisted, linked, through lengths and breadths
Of time. Snow fell, undated. Light
Each summer thronged the glass. A bright
Litter of birdcalls strewed the same
Bone-riddled ground. And up the paths
The endless altered people came,

Washing at their identity.
Now, helpless in the hollow of
An unarmorial age, a trough
Of smoke in slow suspended skeins
Above their scrap of history,
Only an attitude remains:

Time has transfigured them into
Untruth. The stone fidelity
They hardly meant has come to be
Their final blazon, and to prove
Our almost-instinct almost true:
What will survive of us is love.

It was the Irish poet Seamus Heaney who brought archaeology into the centre of twentieth-century poetry. His so-called 'Bog' poems (initially drawing on his reading of P. V. Glob's Scandinavian work on bog corpses) started it off; and since then Heaney, Nobel laureate, has gone on to refine and strengthen his delvings. One of the poems which derives, initially, most directly from Glob's work comes from Heaney's book *North* (1975):

Punishment

I can feel the tug
of the halter at the nape
of her neck, the wind
on her naked front.

It blows her nipples
to amber beads,
it shakes the frail rigging
of her ribs.

I can see her drowned
body in the bog,
the weighing stone,
the floating rods and boughs.

Under which at first
she was a barked sapling
that is dug up
oak-bone, brain-firkin:

her shaved head
like a stubble of black corn,

her blindfold a soiled bandage,
her noose a ring

to store
the memories of love.
Little adulteress,
before they punished you

you were flaxen-haired,
undernourished, and your
tar-black face was beautiful.
My poor scapegoat,

I almost love you
but would have cast, I know,
the stones of silence.
I am the artful voyeur

of your brain's exposed
and darkened combs,
your muscles' webbing
and all your numbered bones:

I who have stood dumb
when your betraying sisters,
cauled in tar,
wept by the railings,

who would connive
in civilized outrage
yet understand the exact
and tribal, intimate revenge.

When Ted Hughes was an undergraduate at Cambridge in the early 1950s, he switched from English to Archaeology and Anthropology; and though I feel Hughes's anthropological interests were probably stronger than his archaeological ones, there seems to be a strong flavour of what one could call linguistic archaeology in his poem *Thistles*. Remember that Hughes came from a partly Viking enclave of Yorkshire:

Thistles

Against the rubber tongues of cows and the hoeing
                                        hands of men
Thistles spike the summer air
Or crackle open under a blue-black pressure.

Every one a revengeful burst
Of resurrection, a grasped fistful
Of splintered weapons and Icelandic frost thrust up

From the underground stain of a decayed Viking.
They are like pale hair and the gutturals of dialects.
Every one manages a plume of blood.

Then they grow grey, like men.
Mown down, it is a feud. Their sons appear,
Stiff with weapons, fighting back over the same ground.

From Geoffrey Hill, two poems – or rather one early poem, and then a section from a later prose-poem. Hill has a magnificent, cryptic sense of the past, which he developed when he was a very young man. He was only nineteen when he wrote *Merlin*:

Merlin

I will consider the outnumbering dead:
For they are the husks of what was rich seed.
Now, should they come together to be fed,
They would outstrip the locusts' covering tide.

Arthur, Elaine, Mordred; they are all gone
Among the raftered galleries of bone.
By the long barrows of Logres they are made one,
And over their city stands the pinnacled corn.

Hill's most highly praised work has been his book-length sequence *Mercian Hymns*, an extraordinary juxtaposition of past and present in the West Midlands, bringing together the West Midlands of Offa and of Hill's own childhood in the 1930s. From all the sections of *Mercian Hymns* (1971), I have chosen the first:

Mercian Hymns

I

King of the perennial holly-groves, the riven sand-
stone: overlord of the M5: architect of the his-
toric rampart and ditch, the citadel at Tamworth,
the summer hermitage in Holy Cross: guardian of

the Welsh Bridge and the Iron Bridge: contractor
to the desirable new estates: saltmaster: money-
changer: commissioner for oaths: martyrologist:
the friend of Charlemagne.

'I liked that,' said Offa, 'sing it again.'

　　　　　　　　　　　　　　　　　　Geoffrey Hill

I love that squib which I think Stuart Piggott quotes somewhere:

> For 'tis not verse and 'tis not prose
> But earthenware alone
> It is that ultimately shows
> What man has thought and done.

Stuart Piggott (1910–96) was a very distinguished archaeologist, in particular a prehistorian of Britain, of Europe, of India, and – in a modest but skilful way – a poet. He had an imaginative, historical approach to archaeology, borne out in his work on such pioneers as William Stukeley and on the 'invention' of the Druids in the eighteenth century. He wrote appreciatively and memorably of his admiration for the difficult work of David Jones, as in the following passage about one of Jones's major works, *The Anathemata*:

> In the summer of last year, when in Vienna examining the great national prehistoric collections, I was given the opportunity of seeing for the first time the original of the famous Upper Palaeolithic sculpture usually kept in the museum safe, and known as The Venus of Willendorf. And as I held this numinous figure, the first words flashed into my mind were not technical archaeological reflections on Gravettian *art mobilier* of 20,000 years ago, but a quotation:
>
> > Who were his *gens*-men or had he no *Hausname* yet
> > no *nomen* for his *fecit*-mark
> >   the Master of the Venus?
> > Whose man-hands god-handled the Willendorf stone
> >   before they unbound the last glaciation.

But Piggott could have a light touch too, as in his *Ballade to a Prehistorian*, addressed to V. Gordon Childe, author of *The Dawn of European Civilisation* – a pioneer work, as Piggott genially acknowledges:

Ballade to a Prehistorian

When sounds of verbal conflict fill the air,
And archaeologists, that curious few,
Debate some problem or in turn prepare
To build whole cultures on the slightest clue –
Then, soon or late, is heard the speaker who
Says to the questing novice – shy, forlorn
And diffident – 'I can't explain to you;
You'll find it in a footnote in "The Dawn".'

Are Frankfort's views of Erösd really fair
And what says Peet of Anghelu Ruju?
What kind of necklace did the Minyans wear
And what did Blegen find at Korakou?
Is Studie o ceském neolithu
The book to read on harpoon-heads of horn?
Is Tallgren's Fatyanovo theory true?
You'll find it in a footnote in 'The Dawn'.

All secrets of the past are here laid bare –
What beer the Beaker folk were wont to brew,
The answer to a Laustitz maiden's prayer,
The recipe for Maglemose fish-glue,
The style of beards the Michelsbergers grew,
The songs they sang when gathering in the corn
At harvest-homes in Late Danubian II –
You'll find it in a footnote in 'The Dawn'.

Envoi

Prince (to your learning be all honour due!)
How will eternity treat man, its pawn?
Leaving the past, do you then turn and view
Man's end as but a footnote to his dawn?

Piggott has a similar light touch, but suggestions of pathos too, in his *Congress of Archaeological Societies*:

Congress of Archaeological Societies

This is the antiquaries' day, they have gathered in London –
Leaving the museum in the quiet country town,
The gaunt rectory, dank amid rook-haunted elms:
The Georgian manor, stuccoed and pedimented;
Dusty lawyer's office, discreet cathedral close.

Sipping tea after the meeting, eagerly reaching for biscuits,
Faces flushed, voices high in querulous debate;
Faded eyes that saw Pitt-Rivers and Greenwell
Peer excitedly at the crumbling potsherd
Unwrapped shakily, fingers rustling the tissue.

Huddled together, vaguely afraid, vaguely distrustful
Of the young men who are turning their hobby into
                                            a science –
Conscious that they were the sowers, yet doubting
                                            the harvest,
Watching the end of an age and the unknown beginning:
Once a year the old people see their children.

And then there's another squib, by Agatha Christie, having a dig – if I may use that word – at her husband Max Mallowan during his work in Syria:

> He said: 'I look for agéd pots
> Of prehistoric days,
> And then I measure them in lots
> And lots and lots of ways.
> And then (like you) I start to write.
> My words are twice as long
> As yours, and far more erudite.
> They prove my colleagues wrong!'

Mockery and satire aren't, indeed, absent from some poems about antiquarianism, as we saw much earlier on, in the extracts from James Cawthorn and William Cowper. Much more recently, in 1979, Fleur Adcock took a shrewd look at the ways in which poets lately seem to have been 'using' the past:

Proposal For a Survey

Another poem about a Norfolk church,
a neolithic circle, Hadrian's Wall?
Histories and prehistories: indexes
and bibliographies can't list them all.
A map of Poets' England from the air
could show not only who and when but where.

Aerial photogrammetry's the thing,
using some form of infra-red technique.
Stones that have been so fervently described
surely retain some heat. They needn't speak:
the cunning camera ranging in its flight
will chart their higher temperatures as light.

We'll see the favoured regions all lit up –
the Thames a fiery vein, Cornwall a glow,
Tintagel like an incandescent stud,
most of East Anglia sparkling like Heathrow;
and Shropshire luminous among the best,
with Offa's Dyke in diamonds to the west.

The Lake District will itself be a lake
of patchy brilliance poured along the vales,
with somewhat lesser splashes to the east

across Northumbria and the Yorkshire dales.
Cities and churches, villages and lanes,
will gleam in sparks and streaks and radiant stains.

The lens, of course, will not discriminate
between the venerable and the new;
Stonehenge and Avebury may catch the eye
but Liverpool will have its aura too.
As well as Canterbury there'll be Leeds
and Hull criss-crossed with nets of glittering beads.

Nor will the cool machine be influenced
by literary fashion to reject
any on grounds of quality or taste:
intensity is all it will detect,
mapping in light, for better or for worse,
whatever has been written of in verse.

The dreariness of eighteenth-century odes
will not disqualify a crag, a park,
a country residence; nor will the rant
of satirists leave London in the dark.
All will shine forth. But limits there must be:
borders will not be crossed, nor will the sea.

Let Scotland, Wales and Ireland chart themselves,
as they'd prefer. For us, there's just one doubt:
that medieval England may be dimmed
by age, and all that's earlier blotted out.
X-rays might help. But surely ardent rhyme
will, as it's always claimed, outshine mere time?

Fleur Adcock

By its own power the influence will rise
from sites and settlements deep underground
of those who sang about them while they stood.
Pale phosphorescent glimmers will be found
of epics chanted to pre-Roman tunes
and poems in, instead of about, runes.

One of the most extraordinary 'archaeological' poems of our own time, I think, is U. A. Fanthorpe's *Unfinished Chronicle*. Here she takes the chance discovery of the Sutton Hoo ship-burial site, shortly before the outbreak of the Second World War, and turns it into a mixture of diary entry, ancient chronicle, and rapt meditation:

1. 1938

A slack year on the estate, the men
Hanging about idle. Mrs Pretty set them
To dig the healthy tumps outside the garden.

> In this year the Germans marched
> Into Austria, and they held it.

Basil, the one with the gift, *had a profound feeling*
(Says authority) *for the local soil*. Grew wedded to it.
If e'd ad is bed (says gardener Jack), *e'd ave slept
Out there in the trench*.

> In this year also wise rulers in Europe
> Met at Munich and spoke for peace.

Three mounds opened. Strange things found
In a boatgrave. *I was a green hand*
(Says Jack), *didn't rightly understand
The value of the things*.

2. 1939

In this year Adolf the leader sent men
Into Bohemia, and they held it.

They trenched the highest barrow, found
The bows of a great ship. Experts came,
Under the darkening skies of the world, to see
What hid at Sutton Hoo.

In this year also the men of Italy
Marched into Albania, and they held it.

The archaeologist spoke. *We might*
As well have a bash (said he, being young),
So a bash was what we had.

In the Bull pub at Woodbridge they stayed,
Clever, lanky young men with pre-war haircuts;
Eminent, emeritus now, with their pasts behind them,
Retired, superseded, dead. And the gold
Came out of the earth bright and shining
As the day it went in.

In this year also Adolf the leader
And Benedict the leader swore to keep faith.
Men called it the pact of steel.

The winds of that year blew Redwald's flaked bones
Over the fields of his kingdom. Gold leaf also
Floated away in that weather.
Potent treasures were packed in boxes and tins
Scrounged from chemists and grocers. It was all borne
From the great ship by an elderly Ford

Which ran out of petrol outside the gates
Of the British Museum.

> In this year also the men of Russia swore
> That they would not fight against the Germans.
> Both sides set their hands to it.

Learned clerks counted and cosseted
The awesome things, and they were stacked
In Aldwych underground for the duration.

> In this year also the men of Germany
> Marched into Poland, and they held it.
> Then the rulers of England and France,
> Who were handfast, defied the Germans,
> And there was open war.

Long enough ago.

Now Mrs Pretty is dead, who loyally gave
The royal lot to the nation. Gardener Jack
And brown-fingered Basil died too, no doubt;
We have no records of them. But high to this day
In Londonchester looms the High King's regalia,
Sword, sceptre, shield, helm, drinking horns and harp,
Patched and polished, explained, made innocent, aimless.

Behind glass, air-conditioned, they wait in their own way
For what comes next:
                    another inhumation?
                              another finding?
                                        another year?

U. A. Fanthorpe

Even more recently, in January 2005, I read in the *Times Literary Supplement* what struck me as an excellently evocative poem called *Words at Wharram Percy*, by Peter Didsbury – a very good poet, born in 1946, who for years has earned his living as a small-finds specialist in Roman, medieval and post-medieval pottery. In this poem, he looks – and listens – at one of the most notable deserted-village sites, in East Yorkshire. This, I hope, partly covers what some people may think has been a gap in this book: why nothing about Oliver Goldsmith's long poem *The Deserted Village*? My feeling is that that fine poem of 1770 has little or nothing to do with either antiquarianism or archaeology – at least not in the sense that that great loss to 'deserted village' sites, John Hurst, would have understood it. (John Hurst was one of the pioneer excavators of Wharram Percy):

Words at Wharram Percy

No silence here.
The place is loud with peace.
Blackcap and robin
give voice in the soft June rain,
conspire in their different octaves
with leaf and lawn and stone.
The air retains
millennia of sound. Listen.
An axe-note falls through countless autumns
down the valley's terraced side.
A wife calls out, in Middle English,
to a man who mows in the glebe,
but his blade lisps on as though he has not heard.
Shadow crawls slowly around a mass-dial

scratched on the porch of the church,
dislodging a grain of sand
which falls ringing onto the path.
There is only utterance.
Low-skimming birds pick flies from the tensile
surface of the pond, and each touch rings
as if struck from a vanished bell.
Hillside pasture lies fizzing under the rain,
through which a partridge
hurries her brood to safety
among cowslip, oat grass, Yorkshire fog, black medick.

When I look through my own 'archaeological' poems, I find they stretch back at least fifty-five years – but I'm not going to delve back nearly as far as that. One of the earliest I can remember was written during my army posting near Leptis Magna in 1950. It's a sonorous piece, heavily influenced by my homage to George Barker's poetry, is called *African Elegy*, and was I think the first poem of mine to be published outside the school literary magazine – in Howard Sergeant's *Outposts* (where Kingsley Amis and Alan Sillitoe also first appeared) in early 1952.

The first I want to include was written soon after my return from my second stay in Libya, in 1967, just after the June War. In the winter vacation from the university in Benghazi in 1966, my wife and I with two of our daughters visited Egypt for the first time, staying both in Cairo and in the Valley of the Kings. Back in England, I revisited the Egyptian section in the British Museum. A poem with which I had fruitlessly been struggling suddenly took on an array of 'Egyptian' imagery. In the poem that resulted, imagine some Pharaoh, hitherto undiscovered, lying deep in his magnificent tomb in Upper Egypt, talking to the archaeologist who is trying to find him. But it is also, I think, a poem about the buried or hidden self – something to do with the poem with which earlier I had been struggling in vain:

Monologue in the Valley of the Kings

> I have hidden something in the inner chamber
> And sealed the lid of the sarcophagus
> And levered a granite boulder against the door
> And the debris has covered it so perfectly
> That though you walk over it daily you never suspect.

Every day you sweat down that shaft, seeing on the walls
The paintings that convince you I am at home, living there.
But that is a blind alley, a false entrance
Flanked by a room with a few bits of junk
Nicely displayed, conventionally chosen.
The throne is quaint but commonplace, the jewels inferior,
The decorated panels not of the best period,
Though enough is there to satisfy curators.

But the inner chamber enshrines the true essence.
Do not be disappointed when I tell you
You will never find it: the authentic phoenix in gold,
The muslin soaked in herbs from recipes
No one remembers, the intricate ornaments,
And above all the copious literatures inscribed
On ivory and papyrus, the distilled wisdom
Of priests, physicians, poets and gods,
Ensuring my immortality. Though even if you found them
You would look in vain for the key, since all are in cipher
And the key is in my skull.

The key is in my skull. If you found your way
Into this chamber, you would find this last:
My skull. But first you would have to search the others,
My kinsfolk neatly parcelled, twenty-seven of them
Disintegrating in their various ways.
A woman from whose face the spices have pushed away
The delicate flaking skin: a man whose body
Seems dipped in clotted black tar, his head detached:
A hand broken through the cerements, protesting:
Mouths in rigid grins or soundless screams –
A catalogue of declensions.

Anthony Thwaite

How, then, do I survive? Gagged in my winding cloths,
The four brown roses withered on my chest
Leaving a purple stain, how am I different
In transcending these little circumstances?
Supposing that with uncustomary skill
You penetrated the chamber, granite, seals,
Dragged out the treasure gloatingly, distinguished
My twenty-seven sorry relatives,
Labelled them, swept and measured everything
Except this one sarcophagus, leaving that
Until the very end: supposing then
You lifted me out carefully under the arc-lamps,
Noting the gold fingernails, the unearthly smell
Of preservation – would you not tremble
At the thought of who this might be? So you would steady
Your hands a moment, like a man taking aim, and lift
The mask.

              But this hypothesis is absurd. I have told you already
You will never find it. Daily you walk about
Over the rubble, peer down the long shaft
That leads nowhere, make your notations, add
Another appendix to your laborious work.
When you die, decently cremated, made proper
By the Registrar of Births and Deaths, given by *The Times*
Your six-inch obituary, I shall perhaps
Have a chance to talk with you. Until then, I hear
Your footsteps over my head as I lie and think
Of what I have hidden here, perfect and safe.

During that second time in Libya, I often went to the exiguous remains of Euhesperides, on the edge of Benghazi: the site of a Greek settlement which seems to have existed between the sixth century BC and about the middle of the third century BC, when it was abandoned. Half lies under a now-disused Islamic cemetery, half under wasteland which in the mid-1960s was an unofficial city rubbish dump. (It is now, all of it, ostensibly 'protected'.) This is the setting of my poem *The Return*, which I wrote in the late 1980s, in England, soon after the incident which is referred to half-way through the poem. Indeed, all that is left of the object is a small dish with a thin dump of ash:

The Return

I picked her up that hot sand-blasted day
In Euhesperides – a rubbish tip
Where all Benghazi's refuse piled across
Scatterings of a millennium of mess:
A broken head of earthenware, a face
Staring out silently, wreathed in her dress
Of fragile terracotta. Picked her up
And brought her home, and meant to let her stay.
She lodged there in a cabinet, and moved
As we moved, to this other place, and lay
For twenty years in England.

                        Till today
I looked inside the cabinet, observed
The spilth of dust and splinters at her neck,
A fallen garment. As I gently took
Her head within my hands, she split and broke,
Her chaplet and her vestiges of dress

Shivering to sand.
                    I threw her all away
Onto the flowerbed: all of her except
The one remaining scrap, her oval face
Lying within my palm. I have it here,
This small masked relic. In this chilly year
The northern damps had killed her where she slept –

The last frail remnant of Persephone,
Whose head it was, whom I picked up that day
After so many broken centuries,
Miraculous and lasting testimony
Among the camel corpses, salt, tins, glass,
And brought her home to live here, till today
She went back to the underworld, as dust.

Her tiny face looks up, and will not last.

I suppose it must have been in 1995 or 1996, when I was working on the imported stoneware pottery excavated from the Castle Mall ditches in Norwich, that the poem *Archaeology* came to me. One is so aware these days of the jolly facetiousness associated with archaeology – a facetiousness bred as much by archaeologists as by those outside the profession: 'Archaeology: A Career in Ruins' and 'Archaeology: A Load of Rubbish'. And there are all those busy, scampering programmes on television, in which the profession seems to be divided between (a) fast-talking presenters who appear to do everything at the double (b) enormously burly, hairy men in trenches, and (c) women who persistently peer through microscopes. Well, each to his or her taste. What I like is scavenging. And *Archaeology* is, perhaps, an attempt to come to terms with what that means:

Archaeology

How would it be if we remembered nothing
Except the garbage and the rubbishing,
The takeaways, the throwaways, the takeovers,
The flakes and breakups, the disjected members
Scattered across the landscape, across everything?

Nothing stands up, nothing stands clear and whole,
Everything bits and pieces, all gone stale,
All to the tip, the midden topped up high
With what we used, with what we threw away:
How would it be if this was all we could feel?

That will not be. Remembering, or feeling,
Or knowing anything of anything,
Will be the last we know of all this stuff.
It will be there for others, seekers of
Things that remain of us, who then are nothing.

Finally, a poem which I hope may catch the essence of what I've been up to in *The Ruins of Time*. Again, it's a poem which had its origin in my second experience in Libya, in the 1960s. But I think it can stand witness to (in the sense Wordsworth meant) 'emotion recollected in tranquillity'. The sherd was picked up in Euhesperides in the 1960s. Years later, I rediscover it. And then, in time, it becomes this poem – a poem which is itself about memory and discovery and rediscovery:

Sigma

Unable to get on with anything,
Throwing out papers, fiddling with piled mess,
I pull a box of sherds out, stacked up here
Among the whole accumulation, less
Because I want to but because it's there –
A scattering of pottery I picked up
Among the Libyan middens I knew once,
And rake it over, chucking out here a cup-
handle, broken, and a flaking rim:
And, in among it all, there's suddenly
This scrap that carries a graffito – Σ
A sigma, a scratched *ess*; and try to tell
Where it once fitted – as beginning or end,
As some abbreviated syllable,
Or sign of ownership, or just a scribble
Made on a day in 450 BC
By someone else who messed about like this,
Unable to get on with anything,
But made his mark for someone else to see.

Postscript

This collection is based on a talk I gave in Burlington House to the Society of Antiquaries of London. It was called 'Poetry, Archaeology and Antiquarianism: a commentary and a reading', and the audience – Fellows of the Society of Antiquaries – seemed to enjoy it. I welcomed Barnaby Rogerson's invitation to turn it into this collection, adding several poems which would have made me over-run the allotted time for the talk.

Although I have earned my living as a writer, editor and teacher, my involvement with archaeology and antiquarianism goes back a long way. My father was a great reader of history, and in my pre-war childhood we were always going off to castles and churches and museums. I had a 'museum' from a very early age. When people have asked me, in interviews, or just in conversation, about *when* I began to be interested in archaeology, my stock reply has been: on my seventh birthday, when my favourite uncle gave me a Roman silver denarius. But I know really that that can't be the beginning, because Uncle Walton wouldn't have given me such a thing without knowing I'd want it.

I can't remember a time when I didn't collect things, but I think that bits of the past – fossils, pieces of old pottery, coins – were certainly in the ascendant by the time I left for America, a wartime evacuee, when I was ten. Fairfax County, Virginia – the place we lived in from late 1940 until some time in 1942 – had some Confederate trenches, or remains of them, from the Civil War; I spent hours there, when I wasn't looking for snakes, looking for musketballs.

Back in England, at Kingswood School in Rutland in 1944, I plunged straight into archaeology. The school had an archaeological society, which I joined, and at the age of fourteen I volunteered to give, and gave, a lecture to the society on 'The

Archaeology of Rutland'. Before long I was Junior Secretary of the society, and then Senior Secretary. (It's always amused me that *my* Junior Secretary was David Wilson – now *Sir* David Wilson, who later became a distinguished archaeologist and Director of the British Museum).

While the school was still in Rutland, I helped to organise a dig in a Saxon cemetery in Glaston, a village close by. And when the school returned to its proper quarters in Bath in 1946, I was helping run another dig at a Roman villa site on Lansdown nearby.

During my compulsory army service, I spent some time attached to a Royal Artillery unit in Libya (which was under British Military Administration, before independence in December 1951), only a mile from the great ruins of a Roman colonial city, Leptis Magna. That was a huge revelation to me, both as an aspirant archaeologist and as an aspirant poet. I spent hours and hours walking through it, foraging in it, usually by myself – no tourists or anything like that. Great columns, and theatres, and temples, and harbours crumbling into the Mediterranean. Early on, I began to find what turned out to be a hoard of Roman coins – 7,800 of them, eventually – in a rock pool by the shore. (I handed them over, dutifully, to the museum in Tripoli which was going to be the national museum of Libya; and they lost them . . .)

During that period of army service in Tripolitania, I worked as a volunteer on local leave with Olwen Brogan and David Oates on a Roman olive-farm site. Later, when I returned to Libya in 1965–67, to teach at the University of Libya in Benghazi, I got to know the Greek Pentapolis: Euhesperides/Berenike, Tauchira, Ptolmeita, Cyrene and Apollonia. Much later still, I spent five weeks in Benghazi in the spring of 2003, working (chiefly on the small finds, mainly pottery) with The Society for Libyan Studies Euhesperides Expedition; and another fortnight in the spring of 2006.

Closer to home, I worked as a volunteer on the Morning-thorpe Anglo-Saxon cemetery site in Norfolk in 1975, and in the 1990s on the imported stoneware pottery from the Castle Mall site in Norwich. In 1998, the Sainsbury Centre in Norwich put on an exhibition, *A Poet's Pots* (their title, not mine), in the Elizabeth Fry Building. I was delighted to be proposed and elected a Fellow of the Society of Antiquaries in 2000. I am a founder member of both the Society for Post-Medieval Archaeology and The Society for Libyan Studies, and a member of the Medieval Pottery Research Group.

Perhaps my one substantial contribution in all this has been an article called *The Chronology of the Bellarmine Jug*, which was published in the April 1973 issue of *The Connoisseur*. It always immodestly delights me to see this cited, as it has been and occasionally still is in archaeological and ceramic history publications: to come across such directions as 'see Thwaite, 1973' or (best of all) 'one must agree with Thwaite' gives me a curious, almost furtive pleasure, of a quite different sort from being represented by my poems in journals or books or anthologies.

Altogether, I think of myself as an archaeologist *manqué*. So this book is, in a way, an attempt at reparation.

ANTHONY THWAITE

Index of First Lines

Against the rubber tongues of cows and the hoeing
      hands of men 46
A slack year on the estate, the men 56
Another poem about a Norfolk church 53
For 'tis not verse and 'tis not prose 49
From school to Cam or Isis, and thence home 17
He said: 'I look for agéd pots 52
He slept beneath his mound of earth 30
How would it be if we remembered nothing 67
I can feel the tug 44
I have hidden something in the inner chamber 61
I met a traveller from an antique land 19
I picked her up that hot sand-blasted day 64
I traced the Circus whose gray stones incline 27
I will consider the outnumbering dead 47
In this year Adolf the leader sent men 57
It chauncéd me oneday beside the shore 12
King of the perennial holly-groves, the riven sand- 47
Legate, I had the news last night – my cohort ordered home 36
No silence here 59
Now profitless the relics that we cull 24
On Wenlock Edge the wood's in trouble 29
Over the heather the wet wind blows 41
Pile of Stone-henge! so proud to hint yet keep 23
Rome disappoints me still; but I shrink and adapt 25
Side by side, their faces blurred 42

The next, a critic, grave and big 15
They have taken the gable from the roof of clay 34
This is the antiquaries' day, they have gathered in London 51
this little piece 15
Thou still unravish'd bride of quietness, 20
Unable to get on with anything 69
Well-wrought this wall: Weirds broke it 10
What matter makes my spade for tears or mirth 35
When Julius Fabricius, Sub-Prefect of the Weald 38
When sounds of verbal conflict fill the air 50

Index of First Lines

Index of Poem Titles

Archaeology   67

Arundel Tomb, An   42

Ballade to a Prehistorian   50

Congress of Archaeological
   Societies   51

Digging   35

In the Old Theatre,
   Fiesole   27

Land, The   38

Mercian Hymns   47

Merlin   47

Monologue in the Valley of
   the Kings   61

Ode on a Grecian Urn   20

On Wenlock Edge   29

Ozymandias   19

Progress of Error, The   17

Proposal For A Survey   53

Punishment   44

Return, The   64

Roman Antiquities   24

Roman Centurion's Song,
   The   36

Roman Wall Blues   41

Ruin, The   10

Ruines of Time, The   12

Selibra Cineris Coacta
   Cani   30

Sigma   69

Swedes   34

Thistles   46

Unfinished Chronicle   56

Words at Wharram Percy   59

Acknowledgements

We would like to thank all those poets and copyright holders who kindly granted us permission to reprint their verses:

Faber & Faber, for permission to reprint *Roman Wall Blues* by W. H. Auden, *Punishment* by Seamus Heaney, *Thistles* by Ted Hughes and *An Arundel Tomb* by Philip Larkin; Penguin Books Ltd, for permission to reprint *Merlin* and *Mercian Hymns: I* by Geoffrey Hill; The Society of Authors, as the literary representative of the estate of A. E. Housman, for *On Wenlock Edge*; Alison M. Sanderson and Stewart F. Sanderson, for poems by Stuart Piggott; Fleur Adcock, for *Proposal for a Survey* from *Poems 1960–2000*, published by Bloodaxe Books; U. A. Fanthorpe, for *Unfinished Chronicle*, from *Collected Poems 1976-2003*, published by Peterloo Poets; Peter Didsbury, for *Words from Wharram Percy*; Enitharmon Press, for poems by Anthony Thwaite, from *Selected Poems 1956–1996* and *A Move in the Weather*.

In addition, Anthony Thwaite would like to thank Dr R. V. Bailey, Jeremy Crow, Duncan McArdle and Professor Charles Thomas for advice and help, and Dr David Gaimster, General Secretary of The Society of Antiquaries.

This pocket book of poetry is part of a growing Poetry of Place series, published by Eland. Other titles in the series:

London
Desert Air
Venice

Forthcoming titles:
Paris
Andalucia
Istanbul
The Highlands

If you would like to receive our detailed catalogue, please contact us at:

Eland Publishing Ltd
61 Exmouth Market, London EC1R 4QL
Tel: 020 7833 0762   Fax: 020 7833 4434
E-mail: info@travelbooks.co.uk
www.travelbooks.co.uk